Live Simply

Gluten Free Recipes for a Healthy Lifestyle

Frances E. Weller

DEDICATION

This book is dedicated to my niece Amanda. May you walk in good health and never look back.

ACKNOWLEDGMENTS

To my husband Doug and son Weston. Thank-you for trying all of the recipes especially the ones that were not included in this book! I appreciate all the computer help and your incredible love and patience. I love you.

To our friend Mark Mespelt, thank-you for taking an evening and doing a photo shoot for the Cookbook. Your photography skills are terrific.

BIO

Frances was born in British Columbia, Canada and took her training as a Combined Lab and X-Ray Technician in Saskatoon, Saskatchewan, graduating in 1980. She did her Pre-Med in Dawson Creek British Columbia, graduating in 1990 with Honors as a Medical Laboratory Technologist in Kamloops, British Columbia. After moving to California in 1990, she graduated with a degree in Hospital Administration from Saint Mary's College in Moraga, CA in 1994. Frances enjoys cooking and also likes being creative in Card making and Scrapbooking. Bike riding in Monterey, CA is one of her favorite activities. She also enjoys working out at the gym. Frances met her husband Doug in California and they were married in September of 1991. They have one son and make their home in Silicon Valley.

INDEX

My Story   9

A few tips for baking gluten free   12

MUFFINS

Banana Oatmeal Muffins   15
Blueberry Muffins   16
Oat Bran Muffins   17
Pumpkin Muffins   18
Rice Muffins   19

QUICK BREADS

Cornbread   21
Banana Bread   22
Baking Powder Biscuits   23

BREAKFAST DISHES

Baked Oatmeal   25
Simply Divine Oatmeal   26
Crepes   27
Pancakes   28
Buckwheat Pancakes   29

SWEET TREATS

Ginger Snap Cookies   31
Carrot Cake   32
Homemade Graham Crackers   33
 or Cut-out Cookies
Apple Oat Balls   35
Fruit Crisp   36
Orange Sponge Cake   37
Oatmeal Cookies   38

SNACKS

Kale Chips   41
Chex Mix   42

SOUP

Salmon Chowder   45
Lentil Soup   46
Hamburger Soup   47
Chicken Soup   48
Turkey Soup   49
Vegetable Soup   50

MEAT/MAIN DISHES

Orange Chicken	53
Honey-Garlic Chicken	54
Easy-Baked Chicken	55
Brown Rice with Ground Beef	56
Turkey Lasagna	57
Baked Salmon	59
Pan Fried Fish	60
Baked Fish	61

VEGETABLES

Stir-Fried Cabbage	63
Sweet Potato/Yam Fries	64
Oven Roasted Potatoes	65
Stir-Fried Vegetables	66
Steamed Vegetables	67
Roasted Vegetables	68

SALADS

Red Potato Salad	71
Chicken Salad	72
Coleslaw	73
Vegetable Salad	74
Ambrosia Salad	75

SALAD DRESSINGS AND CROUTONS

Orange Vinaigrette   77
Homemade Ranch Dressing or Dip   78
Lemon Avocado Dressing   79
Yogurt Basil Dressing   80
Homemade Croutons   81

SIDE DISHES

Rice or quinoa Pilaf   83

SAUCES/SEASONINGS/MARINADES

Sweet and Sour Sauce   85
Gravy   86
Homemade Taco Seasoning   87
Steak Marinade   88
Cranberry/Orange Sauce   89

MY STORY

Each day is part of the journey of life – even ordinary days.

I am so thankful for just an ordinary day as for many years my days were anything but ordinary. In 2006, after twenty years of countless doctor visits with numerous specialists to try and uncover the cause of extreme fatigue, digestive problems, unexplained aches and pains, multiple miscarriages and many food allergies, I was diagnosed with Lyme disease. I was very grateful to finally have a diagnosis and realize that bacteria were causing my multiple health problems and I was not losing my mind!

However, I continued to struggle with my health, trying desperately to find enough foods to eat that my body would not react to. My immune system was on high alert and reacted to most everything. I struggled with joint pain, insomnia, anxiety and weight loss continued to plague me.

I went to my Endocrinologist and told him about the problems I continued to have and he recommended I go totally gluten free, not to eat even a crumb of gluten for six weeks. Gradually, over time I began to notice an improvement in my health. I noticed that the pain in my right side was no longer there and I did not feel that deep fatigue that seemed to go right to my core. I had more energy and my body seemed to be not as sensitive to everything anymore. I was amazed. Going gluten free was definitely worth it!

Over the years I have read many books, taken courses and studied as much research as I could on gluten sensitivity, celiac disease, Lyme disease, nutrition and even cancer. With my background in the Medical Field, I am passionate about health and especially about nutrition. What we put in our mouth is fundamental to building and maintaining good health.

The benefits of a gluten free diet are tremendous but there are many other aspects of nutrition to consider. It is not sufficient for optimum health to just replace wheat flour with gluten free flour. A person needs to look at their diet as a whole and how much sugar and artificial additives and preservatives they consume.

Taking care of our bodies takes time and effort but as the old saying goes, "An ounce of prevention is worth a pound of cure."

I have always enjoyed cooking and all the food I eat is homemade. My diet is free from gluten, dairy, soy, sugar, eggs, nuts and preservatives.

Over the past few years I have developed a lot of recipes for myself and my family. Many friends have asked for my recipes so I decided it was time to put them together into a cookbook. The recipes in this book are simple, quick and help build good nutrition.

As I have learned and grown over the years, I have developed a lifestyle that involves every aspect of life— spiritual, emotional and physical. I have found that it is essential to my well-being to eat nutritionally, drink plenty of pure water, get sunshine, fresh air, sufficient sleep, exercise, maintain a positive attitude and most important, a personal, loving relationship with God.

I am so thankful to God for the improvement in my health and thank Him daily for the privilege of living simply and enjoying the ordinary days.

A few tips for baking gluten free

Gluten free flour mix

Rice Flour	2 cups
Potato Starch	2/3 cup
Tapioca Starch	1/3 cup

This mixture can be used to replace any regular flour recipe.
Rice flour can be white or brown preferably brown as it has more fiber and is less refined.

Any gluten free flour can be substituted for the rice flour, such as Buckwheat flour, Oat flour, Sorghum flour, Almond flour or Teff flour. Rice flour and a little Coconut flour give excellent taste and the coconut flour gives a lower glycemic index.

Guar gum or Xanthan gum must be used in every baking recipe to bind the mixture together otherwise the baked good will crumble. The guar gum and xanthan gum are expensive initially but you only use ½ - 1 tsp. in each recipe so they last for a very long time.

If coconut flour is used, watch the liquid as it will require a little more. The following recipes have been adjusted but just be aware of that.

Gluten free flour does not contain any preservatives. Therefore it is important to keep flour mixtures in the refrigerator or freezer.

It is also important to freeze any baked goods or meals within 24 hours in order to preserve freshness. Thaw for several hours at room temperature.

Gluten free products need a little bit of honey or sugar in order to get that nice golden brown top on baked goods. I have reduced the sugar content significantly in all the recipes but have retained a minimum amount of honey or sugar to ensure browning.

Gluten free baking is more fragile than regular wheat flour. Therefore, using parchment paper is very helpful for rolling out dough.

MUFFINS

BANANA OATMEAL MUFFINS

1 ½ cups gluten free flour mix (can substitute ½ cup coconut flour)
1 cup gluten free oatmeal
¼ cup brown sugar or ¼ cup applesauce
2 tsp. baking powder
1 tsp. baking soda
¼ tsp. salt
1 tsp. guar gum or xanthan gum
2 eggs or egg replacer
¼ cup oil
¼ cup milk (can use coconut milk, cultured coconut milk or buttermilk))
3 medium bananas
1 tsp. vanilla

Mix dry ingredients together. Mix wet ingredients together. Combine and mix well.
Spoon into greased muffin tins.
Bake at 400 F.
12-15 minutes for mini muffins
20-25 minutes for regular muffins

BLUEBERRY MUFFINS

½ cup gluten free rolled oats
½ cup orange juice
1 ½ cups gluten free flour mixture (can substitute in ¼ -1/2 cup coconut flour)
¼ cup brown sugar or ¼ cup applesauce and 1 Tbsp. honey
1 ½ tsp. baking powder
¼ tsp. salt
¼ tsp. baking soda
1 tsp. guar gum or xanthan gum
½ cup oil
1 egg beaten or egg replacer
1 cup blueberries

Combine oats and orange juice, stir well. Add egg and oil. Mix dry ingredients, add to other mixture. Spoon into muffin tins. Blend 1 Tbsp. brown sugar and ½ tsp. cinnamon, sprinkle over tops of muffins.
Bake at 400 F
Mini muffins 12-15 minutes
Regular muffins 18-22 minutes until golden.

OAT BRAN MUFFINS

2 cups gluten free oat bran
¼ cup brown sugar (or ¼ cup applesauce and 1 Tbsp. honey)
3 tsp. baking powder
1 tsp. guar gum or xanthan gum
1 tsp. vanilla extract (gf)
1 cup milk (can use coconut milk, cultured coconut milk or buttermilk)
2 eggs or egg replacer
2 Tbsp. honey
2 Tbsp. oil

Mix dry ingredients together. Mix wet ingredients together. Combine wet with dry and mix until blended. Pour into muffin tins.

Bake at 400F
Mini muffins 12-15 minutes
Regular muffins 20-25 minutes

For variation add: ½ cup chopped apple
¼ cup chopped nuts
1 tsp. cinnamon
Or
Add ¼ cup bananas
¼ cup chopped nuts

17

PUMPKIN MUFFINS

1 ¼ cups gluten free flour mix
½ cup coconut flour
¼ cup brown sugar
1 Tbsp. baking powder
¼ tsp. salt
1 tsp. cinnamon
¼ tsp. nutmeg
¼ tsp. cloves
¼ cup raisins (optional)
2/3 cup milk (can use coconut milk, cultured coconut milk or buttermilk)
½ cup pumpkin
1/3 cup vegetable oil
1 egg or egg replacer
½ tsp. guar or xanthan gum

Mix wet ingredients, mix dry ingredients and combine together. Stir until moistened.
Fill muffin cups.
Bake at 400 F
Mini muffins 12-15 minutes
Regular muffins 20-25 minutes

RICE MUFFINS

1 cup brown rice flour
1 Tbsp. tapioca starch
2 tsps. Baking powder
¼ tsp. salt
½ tsp. guar gum or xanthan gum
2 Tbsp. canola oil
2 tsp. honey
¾-1 cup of water

Mix dry ingredients together, mix wet ingredients together. Mix both together and mix until well moistened. Spoon into 6 count muffin tin. Bake at 375 F for about 25-28 minutes until golden brown. (I use non-stick paper muffin cups).

The same recipe can be used for Pancakes just add a little more water to thin batter and cook on a hot griddle.

QUICK BREADS

CORNBREAD

1 cup cornmeal
½ cup gluten free flour mix
½ cup coconut flour
1 Tbsp. baking powder
¼ tsp. salt
1 Tbsp. brown sugar
1 tsp. guar gum or xanthan gum
1 egg
1 cup coconut milk, cultured coconut milk or buttermilk, may need 1/4 to a 1/3 cup more depending on consistency
¼ cup butter or oil

Mix all the dry ingredients together. Beat egg and milk together. Add the butter or oil. Mix dry ingredients with wet ingredients. Stir just enough to mix. Fill greased pans half full. Use small loaf pans or 8x8 square baking dish.
Bake at 425F (220 C) for 20-25 minutes until lightly brown and toothpick comes out clean.

BANANA BREAD

1 ½ cup gluten free flour mixture (can substitute in ½ cup coconut flour)
½ tsp. baking soda
2 tsp. baking powder
3/4 tsp. guar gum or xanthan gum
¼ tsp. salt
1 cup mashed bananas
4 Tbsp. oil
1-2 Tbsp. honey
1 tsp. vanilla

Mix dry ingredients together, mix wet ingredients together. Mix all together.
Pour into greased pan. I use two small loaf pans. If you use 1 large loaf pan it will require more time. Bake at 350 F for 20-25 minutes or until toothpick comes out clean.

BAKING POWDER BISCUITS

1½ cups gluten free flour mix
½ cup coconut flour
1 tsp. Honey
¾ tsp. guar or xanthan gum
¼ tsp. sea salt
1 Tbsp. baking powder
½ cup earth balance margarine or coconut oil
1-1 ½ cups coconut milk or butter milk (cultured coconut milk is great)
Preheat oven to 425F. Line a baking sheet with parchment paper.
Mix dry ingredients together. Cut in margarine or coconut oil with a pastry blender or fork until mixture resembles coarse crumbs. Stir in coconut milk and honey until a dough forms. Knead until dough is well mixed. Flatten on lightly floured parchment paper. Place another piece of parchment paper or wax paper over dough and roll out to about ½ inch thick with a rolling pin.
Cut into squares or use a round cup to make round biscuits. Arrange on parchment lined baking sheet about 1 ½ inches apart. Bake until golden brown, about 15 minutes. Variation: Add 1 tsp. garlic powder and 1 tsp. onion powder to dry ingredients to give a nice savory taste.

BREAKFAST

BAKED OATMEAL

½ cup applesauce
2 Tbsps. honey
1 egg
3 cups gluten free oatmeal
2 tsp. baking powder
¼ tsp. sea salt
1 ½ tsp. cinnamon
1 cup coconut milk (cultured coconut milk is good too)
1 tsp. vanilla
¾ cup blueberries

Combine all the dry ingredients in a large bowl. Mix the wet ingredients in a small bowl. Add the wet ingredients to the dry ingredients. Mix well and gently stir in blueberries.

Pour into lightly greased 8x8 inch glass baking dish.

Bake at 350 f for 40 minutes or until light brown. Serve warm.

SIMPLY DIVINE OATMEAL

2 cups water
1 cup gluten free oatmeal (or ½ cup gluten free oat bran and ½ cup gluten free oatmeal)

In a large pot boil the 2 cups of water. Pour in gluten free oatmeal and turn off heat. Place lid on pot and let cook for about 15 minutes until the water has been absorbed by the oatmeal.

In a cereal bowl add the following:
(This is enough for 1 serving)
1 Tbsp. unsweetened coconut
1 ½ Tbsp. raisins or sliced dates
Pinch of salt
1 Tbsp. slivered almonds or walnuts (optional)
1 Tbsp. gluten free granola
½ small apple cut in small pieces or ¼ cup blueberries
½ tsp. vanilla extract (gf)
1 tsp. cinnamon

Add ½ of the cooked oatmeal and stir well. Serve immediately.

CREPES

3/4 cup gluten free flour mix

¼ cup coconut flour

1 Tsp. brown sugar

½ tsp. guar gum or xanthan gum

1 Tbsp. melted butter

1 ½ cups cultured coconut milk or unsweetened coconut milk

1 egg

Mix the flour and sugar in a large bowl. Add the coconut milk and egg and beat until the mixture is smooth. Add butter and mix well. If the mixture is too thick add additional coconut milk or water.

Heat a frying pan and grease well. Pour a 1/4 cup of the batter into the pan and turn the skillet to make a circle with the batter.
Cook the crepe until it is light brown. Flip the crepe with a spatula. Cook the other side of crepe until it is light brown. Place crepe gently on wire cooling rack. Grease pan again and repeat until batter is all used up. The recipe makes about 6 crepes.

Serve with sliced fresh strawberries or other fresh fruit.

PANCAKES

1 egg (optional)
1 cup gluten free flour mix
¾ cup of milk (coconut or almond) or water
2 Tbsp. canola oil
1 ½ tsp. honey
3 tsp. baking powder
¼ tsp. sea salt
¾ tsp. xanthan or guar gum

Mix all the liquid ingredients together and beat well. Add dry ingredients and mix until batter is smooth. Add additional milk or water if too thick. Cook pancakes on hot griddle or frying pan turning when pancakes are puffed up and dry around the edges. Cook until golden brown. Serve warm.

BUCKWHEAT PANCAKES

½ cup buckwheat flour
½ cup gluten free cornmeal
1 ½ tsp. Baking powder
½ tsp. sea salt
¾ tsp. xanthan or guar gum
½ tsp. vanilla extract
1 ½ tsp. honey
1 cup water - cultured or plain coconut milk works well
1 mashed banana
1 egg
Oil spray for skillet

Mix all dry ingredients together.
Mix all liquid ingredients together.
Prepare skillet. Spoon the batter into the skillet with a large tablespoon. Cook quickly on hot skillet, being careful not to burn the pancakes.

If batter seems too thick add additional water or milk. Spray the skillet after each batch.

SWEET TREATS

GINGER SNAP COOKIES

1 ½ cups gluten free flour mixture
½ cup buckwheat flour
2 tsp. baking soda
½ tsp. sea salt
2 tsp. ginger
1 tsp. cinnamon
¼ tsp. cloves

¼ cup water
½ cup oil
1/3 cup molasses
¼ cup honey or 1 Tbsp. honey and ¼ cup applesauce
2 tsp. apple cider vinegar
¼ cup ground flax seed

Combine liquid ingredients and mix well. Combine dry ingredients in a large mixing bowl and mix with dry ingredients.
Drop by spoon onto a baking sheet and press down cookies with a fork. Bake at 350 F for 18-20 minutes.

CARROT CAKE

1 cup gluten free flour
½ cup coconut flour
1 tsp. baking soda
1 tsp. cinnamon
½ tsp. salt
3/4 tsp. guar gum or xanthan gum
1 cup grated carrots (can also substitute grated zucchini)
1 Tbsp. lemon juice
¾ - 1 cup milk, coconut milk or water
1/3 cup oil
1 tsp. vanilla
1 Tbsp. honey

Mix dry ingredients in ungreased 8x8 baking pan, stir until blended. Add remaining ingredients, stir to blend well.
Bake at 350 F
Bake 25-35 minutes until toothpick comes out clean. Cool in pan.

HOMEMADE GRAHAM CRACKERS OR CUT OUT COOKIES

¾ cup earth balance margarine, or coconut oil
¼ cup honey
1/2 cup brown sugar or ½ cup applesauce and ¼ cup brown sugar
1 tsp. vanilla
1 ½ cups gluten free flour mixture
1 cup brown rice flour
½ cup coconut flour
1 tsp. guar gum or xanthan gum
½ tsp. sea salt
1 tsp. cinnamon (optional)
1 Tbsp. baking powder
½ to 1 cup water (if using applesauce try 1/3-1/2 cup of water)

Preheat oven to 325 F. Mix margarine, honey, sugar and vanilla, beat well with mixer. Mix dry ingredients in another bowl. Mix all ingredients together in a mixer. Knead dough until it forms a ball. Refrigerate for at least 1 hour.
Roll dough onto lightly floured parchment paper. Use wax paper or parchment paper on top of dough to prevent sticking to the rolling pin. Roll to about ½ inch thick.   (continued)

For graham crackers cut into squares and prick each square with a fork.

For rolled cookies use cookie cutters.

Bake 18-20 minutes. Don't let them get too brown.

Remove from pan and cool.

APPLE OAT BALLS

½ cup water
1 cup grated apple with peel
¼ cup vegetable oil
1 tsp. vanilla
½ cup chopped walnuts or almonds or sunflower seeds or pumpkin seeds (your choice)
¼ tsp. salt
1 cup gluten free Oat Bran
1 cup chopped dates
2 cups gluten free oats

Preheat oven to 350F
In a saucepan, simmer chopped dates in the water for about 5 minutes. Remove from heat and mash with a fork. Add grated apple and oil and mix until smooth. Add remaining ingredients and mix well.
Let stand 10 minutes. Mix well and form into balls.
Place onto dry baking sheet.
Bake for 20 minutes until lightly browned.

FRUIT CRISP

¼ cup earth balance margarine or coconut oil
1 – 2 Tbsp. brown sugar or honey
1½ cups gluten free oatmeal
1 Tbsp. gluten free flour mixture
1 tsp. cinnamon (optional)
1 tsp. vanilla
Slice fruit (apples/blueberries/peaches/pears etc.)

Mix margarine and sugar. Stir in oatmeal, flour and vanilla. Set aside
Choose any fruit you like. Slice in bottom of glass pie plate. Stir in 2 Tbsps. granulated tapioca and 1 Tbsp. brown sugar or honey. Pour topping on fruit mixture.

Bake at 350 F for 20-30 minutes until fruit is soft and juice is bubbling.

ORANGE SPONGE CAKE

1/3 cup applesauce
¼ cup honey or brown sugar
4 eggs, separated
1 Tbsp. grated orange rind
½ cup fresh orange juice
¾ cup Gluten free flour mixture
¼ cup coconut flour
2 tsp. baking powder
¼ tsp. sea salt
1 tsp. xanthan or guar gum

In a large mixing bowl combine applesauce, honey, egg yolks, orange rind and orange juice, beat well. Add flour, baking powder and xanthan or guar gum. Mix well.
In a separate bowl, combine the egg whites and the salt. Beat until it forms stiff peaks. Gently fold the yolk mixture into the whites.
Pour into an ungreased angel food pan. Bake at 325F for 50 -55 minutes until the cake is golden brown and toothpick comes out clean.
Turn cake upside down and let cool completely before removing it from the pan.
Serve with fresh strawberries or blueberries.

OATMEAL COOKIES

½ cup butter or earth balance margarine
½ cup apple sauce
1 Tbsp. honey
1 egg or egg replacer
2 tsp. vanilla extract
½ tsp. sea salt
½ cup unsweetened coconut (chocolate chips, dried cranberries or raisins could also be used)
½ cup sunflower seed or almonds (optional)
1 cup gluten free rolled oats
1 cup gluten free flour mix
1 tsp. baking powder
1 tsp. xanthan or guar gum

Preheat oven to 325F. Line a baking sheet with parchment paper. Mix dry ingredients in a large bowl. In a separate bowl mix the softened butter, egg, applesauce, honey and vanilla extract, beat until well combined.

Drop by tablespoon onto baking sheets spacing 2 inched apart and press down with a fork. Bake until lightly browned, about 10-12 minutes.

SNACKS

KALE CHIPS

Take any variety of Kale and wash well. Pat dry and separate leaves from spine. Place on parchment paper on an ungreased cookie sheet. Sprinkle with olive oil and sea salt.

Bake at 275F for about 20 minutes until Kale is dried. Turn occasionally. Remove from oven and cool. Delicious and nutritious!

CHEX-MIX   Oven Method

3 cups gluten free corn cereal squares
3 cups gluten free rice cereal squares
2 cups gluten free toasted O's
2 cups gluten free pretzels
1 cup nuts (optional)

3 Tbsp. butter or coconut oil
1 ½ Tbsp. Worcestershire sauce
1 tsp. gluten and MSG free season salt
1 tsp. garlic powder
½ tsp. onion powder

Heat oven to 250 F. In a large bowl, mix the cereal and the pretzels, set aside. In an ungreased large roasting pan, melt butter or coconut oil in the oven. Stir in seasonings. Gradually stir in the cereal mixture until evenly coated. Bake 1 hour, stirring every 15 minutes. Spread on paper towels to cool, about 15 minutes.

SOUP

SALMON CHOWDER

2 Tbsp. coconut oil
1 onion chopped
2 green onions chopped
1 green pepper, chopped
1 small garlic clove
1 can (14.5 oz.) diced tomatoes
1 cup chicken broth
1 tsp. basil

Saute' veggies, add about ½-1 cup flaked fresh or frozen cooked wild salmon or 1 can of wild salmon. Bring to boil, reduce heat, simmer 10 minutes. Can also add ½ a cup of cooked brown rice to make a hearty chowder.

I often add additional vegetables like carrots, baby Bok Choy, etc.

LENTIL SOUP

2 medium onions – chopped
1 large green pepper – chopped
2 Tbsp. coconut oil
Saute' above ingredients until tender

1 ½ cups lentils
4 cups of water or vegetable broth
1 – 28 oz. can tomatoes
2 large carrots – sliced
1 tsp. basil
¼ tsp. sea salt
¼ tsp. pepper (optional)

Bring to boil then lower heat, cover and simmer about 45 minutes, until lentils and vegetables are tender.

Serves 6.

HAMBURGER SOUP

1 lb. of 100% grass fed ground beef
1 onion, chopped
1 – 28 oz. can of tomatoes
2 cups water
1 can tomato soup (gluten free)
4 carrots, chopped
3 stalks celery, chopped
½ cup brown rice
1 tsp. basil
3 cans beef broth (gluten free)
Salt and pepper to taste

Brown the meat and onions. Combine all
ingredients in a large pot. Cook 1-2 hours or use
crock pot up to 8 hours.
Serves 10-12. Freezes well.

Variation: Add 1 tsp. taco seasoning (gf) or 1 tsp.
chili powder. You can add as many vegetables as
you like.

Substitute ground Turkey for ground beef and
chicken broth for the beef broth.

CHICKEN SOUP

Boil left over chicken bones from roast chicken.
Place chicken bones in a large pot and cover with
water. Boil for 3 – 4 hours stirring occasionally.
Remove bones from broth and take the meat off
the bones and place in broth.

Add the following ingredients to the broth and
meat:
2-4 stalks of celery, chopped
1 onion, chopped
2-4 carrots, chopped
½ package of cut frozen green beans or 1 cup of
fresh green beans cut into pieces
1 cup of brown rice noodles or ½ cup short grain
brown rice
1 tsp. season salt
1 Tbsp. basil
1 ½ tsp. garlic powder
1 ½ tsp. onion powder

Bring all to a boil and then turn to simmer for 25-30
minutes. Stir occasionally.
Add baby Bok Choy or kale for additional flavor and
vegetables. Serve hot.

TURKEY SOUP

Same recipe as Chicken soup except substitute turkey bones for chicken bones. Follow recipe as written for Chicken soup.

VEGETABLE SOUP

1 (14 oz.) can diced tomatoes
1   32 oz. container low sodium gluten free
      vegetable broth
1 (14 oz.) can chicken broth
1 onion, chopped
2 cloves garlic
2 carrots - sliced
2 celery stalks – sliced
½ head green cabbage – chopped
½ head purple cabbage – chopped
½ head cauliflower – chopped
2 stalks broccoli – chopped
1 ½ tsp. MSG free season salt
1 ½ tsp. garlic powder
1 tsp. onion powder
1 Tbsp. basil
¾ cup brown rice

Saute' onion and garlic in 1 Tbsp. extra virgin
organic coconut oil. Add can of diced tomatoes,
chicken broth and vegetable broth. Bring to a
boil. Add brown rice and reduce heat. Cover and
simmer for 30 minutes. Add vegetables and
simmer for another 30 minutes. Add 1 Tbsp. olive

oil during last 5 minutes of simmering. Stir well and serve warm.

Variation: Add any other vegetables you like. Brussels sprouts, asparagus etc.

MEAT/MAIN DISHES

ORANGE CHICKEN

1 ½ lbs. chicken (cut into 2 inch chunks)
½ cup gluten free flour mix
Coconut oil for browning chicken
½ tsp. sea salt
6 ozs. Orange juice
1 Tbsp. brown sugar
1 tsp. balsamic vinegar
3 Tbsp. ketchup

Coat chicken in gluten free flour, lightly brown in coconut oil. Mix other ingredients well and add chicken. Place mixture in crockpot and cook on High for 3-4 hours. Or return lightly browned chicken and sauce to frying pan and simmer until chicken is tender about 30 minutes. Serve over steamed brown rice.

HONEY GARLIC CHICKEN

1 tsp. garlic powder
1 Tbsp. brown sugar
¼ cup gluten free soy sauce
2 Tbsp. honey

Lay cut up chicken in a pan. Spread with sauce.
Cover and bake at 350 F for 1 ½ hours. Uncover for
the last 10 minutes. Serve with brown rice.

EASY BAKED CHICKEN

Take one free range chicken and wash well with water. Pat dry and place in roasting pan. Roast at 350 F for 1½ hours. Remove from oven and let rest for 10 minutes. Carve and serve. Serve with season salt.

BROWN RICE WITH GROUND BEEF – OR GROUND TURKEY

1/3 lb. ground meat
1 cup chopped onion
2 cups cooked brown rice

Saute' onions in 1 Tbsp. coconut oil. Add the ground meat and stir until cooked. Add the rice and 2 Tbsp. ketchup and ¼ tsp. salt. Sir until rice is browned. Serves 2.

TURKEY LASAGNA

1 lb. ground turkey
½ lb. turkey sausage (all natural without preservatives)
1 onion, chopped
2 cloves garlic, crushed
1 (28 oz.) can of crushed tomatoes
2 (6 oz.) cans of tomato paste
2 (6 oz.) cans of tomato sauce
2 tsps. ground basil
1 tsp. Italian seasoning
12 gluten free lasagna noodles
1 (16 oz.) carton of 1 % cottage cheese
1 (8 oz.) package of low fat mozzarella cheese
½ cup parmesan cheese

Brown ground turkey and onion in large pot. Add sausage and garlic. Stir in tomatoes, tomato paste, tomato sauce and water. Add basil and Italian seasoning and stir well. Simmer for ½ - 1 hour stirring occasionally.

Cook lasagna noodles in large pot of boiling water for about 5-6 minutes. Drain noodles and place in cool water until ready. (Continued)

Preheat oven to 350 F.

Spread 1½ cups meat sauce on bottom of 7x11 glass pan. Arrange 3 noodles over sauce. Spread 4 oz. cottage cheese over noodles and sprinkle with mozzarella cheese and parmesan cheese. Repeat layers and finish with left over mozzarella and parmesan cheese. Place foil over lasagna to form a tent so foil does not touch cheese.

Bake for 25 to 30 minutes. Remove foil and bake for another 20-25 minutes until cheese is melted and lasagna is bubbling. Let cool 15 minutes before serving. Makes 2 pans of lasagna.

BAKED SALMON

Fresh Wild Salmon Fillet

Take fillet and wash well under running water. Place in glass pan skin side down.

Bake at 350 F for 15-20 minutes. Check at 15 minutes. Remove from oven and serve with fresh lemon. Season salt also goes well on salmon after it is cooked. Simple, but delicious.

PAN FRIED FISH

Take any fillet of fish and wash well in running water. Place in a frying pan skin side down on low medium heat. Cover with a tight lid and cook on medium heat for 10 minutes, lower heat to low and check fish. The fish is done when it flakes easily. If the fish is not quite cooked you may add a Tbsp. of water so it does not burn on the bottom.

If there is not skin on the fillet, pace 1 Tbsp. coconut oil in pan so fish does not stick.

BAKED FISH

Grease a glass baking dish with 1 Tbsp. extra virgin organic coconut oil. Take any fish fillet and wash well in running water. Place in lightly greased dish. Sprinkle fish with garlic powder, dill, MSG free season salt and the juice of ½ a fresh lemon.

Bake at 350 F for 15-20 minutes depending on the thickness of the fillet. Fish is cooked when it flakes well. Do not overcook.

Serve with fresh lemon.

VEGETABLES

STIR FRIED CABBAGE

¼ - ½ head of green cabbage
¼ - ½ head of purple cabbage
1 Tbsp. olive oil or coconut oil
Pinch of salt

Lightly heat oil in frying pan or wok. Add cut up cabbage and stir on medium heat. Cover for a few minutes at a time and stir often. Cook until cabbage is tender, about 10-15minutes.

SWEET POTATO / YAM FRIES

Preheat oven to 350 F.

Scrub 1-2 Sweet potatoes or Yams well. Cut into French fries. Place about 1 Tbsp. of olive oil on a cookie sheet, enough oil to lightly cover pan. Spread Sweet Potato or Yam fries on greased cookie sheet so they are not touching each other. Bake for 20 – 25 minutes until lightly browned and tender when tested with a fork.
Turn after 10 minutes.
Serve warm.

OVEN ROASTED POTATOES

Preheat oven to 350 F.

Clean red potatoes and Yukon gold potatoes, do not peel. Cut potatoes into quarters. Place 1 Tbsp. olive oil in bottom of large glass baking pan. Place potatoes in pan and drizzle olive oil over potatoes. Sprinkle with a small amount of sea salt. Bake for 20-30 minutes until nicely browned and tender to a fork, turning often.

Variation: Many spices work good for potatoes. Try Italian seasoning, season salt, garlic powder or onion powder.

STIR FRIED VEGETABLES

Place 1-2 Tbsp. coconut oil in a Stainless steel frying pan or wok. Heat until melted. Lightly stir fry 2 cloves of fresh garlic and 1 chopped onion. Add washed and cleaned vegetables such as:
Carrots
Zucchini
Broccoli
Cauliflower
Bok Choy
Cabbage
Peppers
Celery
Stir fry until just tender when a fork in inserted, about 5-10 minutes. Add garlic powder, onion powder, turmeric and ginger. Add 1 Tbsp. gluten free soy sauce.

Serve over brown rice.

Variations:
Add cut up cooked Chicken, Beef, or Turkey.

STEAMED VEGETABLES

Wash and clean any vegetables and place in steamer over water and steam lightly for 10 minutes.
Serve warm with sea salt and pepper to taste.

ROASTED VEGETABLES

Take a large glass baking dish or a large cookie sheet and cover with a thin layer of olive oil. Clean and wash vegetables such as:

Carrots
Zucchini
Brussels sprouts
Asparagus
Kabocha or butternut squash
Rutabaga

Cut into bite size pieces and place in baking dish. Sprinkle lightly with olive oil and Sea salt or seasoning of choice. Bake in 375F oven for 20 minutes. Turn after 10 minutes. Vegetables are done when tender to a fork. Serve warm.

SALADS

RED POTATO SALAD

6 medium red potatoes
1/3 cup sour cream
½ cup plain yogurt
¼ cup chopped chives or green onions
Salt and pepper

Scrub potatoes. Boil in skins until just fork tender.
Cool and cut into ½ inch cubes.
Combine other ingredients, toss. Refrigerate.
Makes 10, ½ cup servings.

CHICKEN SALAD

2 cups butter or leaf lettuce
3 radishes
1 cucumber
1 small carrot peeled
Any variety of vegetables such as peppers, celery, green onion, avocado
1 cup cut up cooked chicken breast

Combine all ingredients and toss well. Serve with gluten free dressing and gluten free croutons.

COLESLAW

½ head green cabbage
½ head purple cabbage
1 carrot peeled and grated
1 small apple
¼-1/3 cup raisins

Slice cabbage thinly and place in large bowl. Add grated carrot and apple cut into small pieces.
Wash raisins and add to vegetables.
Add 2 Tbsps. gluten free Coleslaw dressing and mix well. Serve.

VEGETABLE SALAD

Lettuce
Cucumber
Grated Carrot
Radish
Red, yellow or green pepper
Avocado
Tomato
Any other raw vegetables you like.

Mix all ingredients together and enjoy with homemade gluten free croutons and dressing.

AMBROSIA SALAD

2 Oranges – peel and cut into cubes
¼ cup organic raisins rinsed in clear water (can also
use cranberries, dried blueberries or dried cherries)
¼ cup unsweetened shredded coconut
Slivered almonds (optional)
Drizzle lightly with honey

Mix all ingredients together and let sit for a few
hours to mix the flavors. Store in the refrigerator.

SALAD DRESSINGS
AND CROUTONS

ORANGE VINAIGRETTE

¼ cup balsamic vinegar
¼ cup extra virgin olive oil
¼ cup fresh orange juice
1½ tsp. Dijon mustard
Pinch of sea salt

Combine all ingredients and mix well. Store in airtight container. Use within 5 days.

HOMEMADE RANCH DRESSING OR DIP

1/3 cup plain Greek style yogurt
1/3 cup buttermilk or cultured coconut milk
3 Tbsp. canola or olive oil mayonnaise
1½ tsps. fresh lemon juice
1 tsp. Dijon mustard
½ tsp. onion powder
½ tsp. garlic powder
1 Tbsp. finely chopped fresh chives (optional)
Pinch of salt

Mix all ingredients together until well combined.
Store in airtight container. Use within 5 days.

LEMON AVOCADO DRESSING

½ ripe avocado
¾ cup buttermilk or cultured coconut milk
1 Tbsp. fresh lemon juice
Pinch of salt
3 Tbsp. fresh parsley well chopped
3 Tbsp. finely chopped fresh chives

Place all ingredients into blender and blend until smooth. Store in airtight container in fridge. Use within 5 days.

YOGURT BASIL DRESSING

¼ cup plain yogurt
¼ cup cottage cheese
½ tsp. dried basil
½ tsp. sugar
2 tsp. lemon juice
Salt and pepper
1 clove of garlic crushed

In blender combine all ingredients, blend until smooth.

HOMEMADE CROUTONS

Take any gluten free bread and butter it on both sides. Place on a cookie sheet and sprinkle well with garlic powder. Cut bread into cubes. Bake in 400F oven for 10-15 minutes until golden brown and crispy. Turn after 5 minutes. Stores well in airtight container in freezer.

SIDE DISHES

RICE OR QUINOA PILAF

1 onion
2 cloves garlic
1 cup sliced mushrooms
1 Tbsp. olive oil
½ tsp. turmeric
1 tsp. MSG-free season salt
1 tsp. garlic powder
1 tsp. onion powder
1 tsp. parsley

In a medium size cooking pot lightly sauté onion, garlic and mushrooms in 1 Tbsp. olive oil. Add 2 cups low sodium chicken broth, vegetable broth or water and 1 cup of brown rice or Quinoa. Bring to a boil and reduce heat to low, add spices and cover. Simmer for 1 hour.
(Note: Rinse Rice or Quinoa in running water and drain well before cooking.)

SAUCES/SEASONINGS /MARINADES

SWEET AND SOUR SAUCE

1 cup apricot puree or fruit juice sweetened jam
1 Tbsp. prepared mustard
¼ cup water
1 tsp. Worcestershire sauce
2 Tbsp. ketchup
2 Tbsp. apple cider vinegar

Mix all ingredients together and pour over cooked meatballs or other meat. Simmer for 15- 20 minutes stirring occasionally.

GRAVY

Take drippings from Chicken, Turkey or Roast Beef and place in saucepan. Mix 2 Tbsp. white rice flour with ½ cup of water. Stir flour mixture into drippings and heat to boiling, stirring continually. Add ¼ tsp. sea salt to taste. If too thick, add a little more water. Garlic and/or onion powder also taste good. Serve.

Variation: Cornstarch, arrowroot powder or tapioca starch can be substituted for the white rice flour.

HOMEMADE TACO SEASONING

1 Tbsp. Chili powder
1 tsp. cumin
1 tsp. onion powder
1 tsp. garlic powder
1 tsp. paprika
½ tsp. oregano

Mix all ingredients together. Store in an airtight glass jar.

STEAK MARINADE

1 Tbsp. gluten free soy sauce
2 Tbsps. extra virgin olive oil
Juice of ½ a fresh lemon
1½ tsp. garlic powder
2 cloves of garlic minced

Mix all ingredients together and marinade steak for several hours. A gallon size zip lock freezer bag works great.
Remove meat and grill on barbeque. Brush with marinade several times during cooking. Let rest 5 minutes before serving.

FRESH CRANBERRY ORANGE SAUCE

1 bag of fresh Cranberries
1 fresh orange
1 Tbsp. orange zest (optional)
¼ cup of honey
1 tsp. cinnamon

Wash cranberries and drain well. Peel orange
and break into sections. Place all ingredients into
a blender and puree until smooth.   Adjust honey
to taste. Store in a tightly covered container in
the fridge. Great with Turkey!

Made in the USA
Las Vegas, NV
13 December 2023

82775030R00055